Adventures Grace

Heather Mortensen

BookLeaf Publishing

India | USA | UK

Presentation by *BookLeaf Publishing*

Web: www.bookleafpub.com

E-mail: info@bookleafpub.com

ISBN: 9789358319071

First edition 2024

miles

Traversing 20,000 miles of winding roads,
Questing for serenity,
Enveloped in the splendor
Of nature's breathtaking artistry,
Discovering solace in cascading tears,
Amidst the embrace of every waterfall
And fragment of my mended heart,
Pressing on,
Never looking back,
Embracing adventures and confronting specters
that lie ahead.

Scenic by ways

Wandering down picturesque byways,
Haunted by cherished memories of a life well
lived,
Silhouettes sway,
In the ethereal embrace of
Redemption's Twilight

Struggle

Losing myself
Or failing to find
Making memories
To eternally bind
A legacy
Of love's embrace
And yesterday's dreams
Or was it tomorrow's grace

Reality

Travel's embrace, a healing balm so wide,
From distant shores to mountainside.
New horizons, new hearts, new grace,
In the journey, finding a healing space.

Quicksand

Time is flimsy, slippery, like water's flow,
Falling through fingers, where does it go?
Stop! Wait! Quicker, faster, slower,
Like quicksand's pull, or magic's allure.

The cascade calls with its sweet song,
A tempting lull, so fierce and strong,
Just like the pull of substance's tide,
It drags the spirit, deep inside.

In the rush of time, the mind does sway,
Seeking solace, a brief delay,
In the fleeting moments, seeking solace,
Lost in the current, a delicate balance.

Yet in the midst of crashing spray,
A glimmer of hope lights the way,
For just as water finds its peace,
The soul can mend, the storms release.

The ebb and flow of life's own dance,
Caught in the current, a fleeting chance,
To break the cycle, to find release,
And let the soul, at last, find peace.

Time is a river, ever-changing,
Slipping through hands, rearranging,
But in its current, there's a chance to find,
A solid ground, a peace of mind.

So as the waterfall crashes down,
Let it wash away the troubled frown,
And in its mist, may clarity appear,
To guide the way, dispelling fear.

For in the rush of time's endless race,
There's a glimmer of hope, a sacred place,
Where addiction's grip can be unbound,
And inner strength and peace are found.

Addiction Falls

Amidst the mist of crashing falls,
A soul stands lost, entwined in thralls,
Addiction's grip, a torrent's might,
A never-ending, ceaseless fight.

Like water rushing o'er the edge,
The urge consumes, a relentless pledge,
To drown in depths of vice's flow,
A downward spiral, endless woe.

The cascade calls with its sweet song,
A tempting lull, so fierce and strong,
Just like the pull of substance's tide,
It drags the spirit, deep inside.

Yet in the midst of crashing spray,
A glimmer of hope lights the way,
For just as water finds its peace,
The soul can mend, the storms release.

So let the falls wash clean the soul,
Renew, refresh, and make it whole,
Break free from chains
And rise above with strength to spare.

Trauma roads

Upon the open road, a healing journey starts,
Where scars of old are soothed by distant hearts.
Beneath the starry sky and mountains tall,
Travel mends the spirit, mends the soul's call.

Through winding paths and cities far and wide,
The traveler finds a place to heal inside.
In every new horizon, a chance to grow,
To leave behind the past, let new stories flow.

Amidst the laughter of strangers, kind and true,
The weight of trauma fades, as friendships
renew.
Each step upon foreign soil, a step toward light,
As travel weaves its magic, dispelling the night.

So let the winds of wanderlust set you free,
Embrace the world's embrace, and find your
glee.
In travel's gentle touch, find strength to cope,
For in the journey's embrace, lies the path to
hope.

Grace and Graves

In the quiet of the graveyard's embrace,
Where time and eternity interlace,
There lies a beauty, a solemn grace,
Where life and death meet face to face.

Beneath the shadow of weathered stones,
Rest the weary souls, the flesh and bones,
Yet in this place, a peace is known,
A grace that lingers, though they've flown.

For in each grave, a story sleeps,
Of joys and sorrows, and secrets deep,
But grace, like ivy, gently creeps,
Binding the memories we'll always keep.

In the hush of twilight, and morning dew,
There's a whisper of grace that breaks anew,
For even in death, it shines right through,
A timeless truth, both old and true.

So let us tread with humble regard,
Where grace and graves stand ever marred,
For in their union, we can discard
The fear of endings, and embrace the starred.

For in the grace that lingers here,
We find a solace, a balm for fear,
A reminder that love's end is near,
But its echoes through time will always steer.

Forgiveness

In the depths of night, where shadows dwell,
A soul adrift in a lonely cell,
Seeking forgiveness, a path to mend,
And in that journey, find yourself, friend.

Through veils of pain and scars of old,
The heartache harbored, the stories untold,
You yearn for light, a soothing balm,
To heal the wounds, to bring you calm.

Forgiveness blooms like a gentle flower,
Softening the edges, releasing the power
Of bitterness and anger's hold,
Unshackling chains, releasing the cold.

As you forgive, you set yourself free,
From the weight of the past, the burdens that be,
And in that freedom, you start to see,
The beauty within, the person to be.

For in forgiveness, a mirror appears,
Reflecting a soul that's weathered the years,
But now with strength and newfound grace,
You rediscover your unique place.

Embracing flaws, and scars of time,
You learn to cherish the mountains you've
climbed,
For in the journey of forgiveness found,
You unearth the treasure of solid ground.

So let forgiveness be your guiding star,
As you navigate life, both near and far,
And in its light, may you come to find,
The peace within, and your truest mind.

Hope waits

In the darkest of nights, when all seems lost,
And shadows engulf the paths we've crossed,
There comes a whisper, a glimmer of light,
A spark in the void, shining so bright.

Hope, once elusive, now stirs and awakes,
Rekindling faith with each step it takes.
Through trials and storms, it perseveres strong,
A melody of courage, a resilient song.

It blooms like a flower in the harshest of lands,
Defying the odds with unwavering hands.
From the depths of despair, it rises anew,
Guiding our hearts to skies clear and blue.

With each sunrise, a promise unfurls,
A tapestry of dreams, unfettered by swirls.
It whispers of journeys yet to unfold,
And treasures of joy, yet to be told.

So let hope's gentle touch mend what's torn,
And kindle the fire that was once worn.
For in hope's embrace, we find our way home,
As it paints the horizon with dreams to roam.

With every heartbeat, a story reborn,
As hope returns, radiant and unadorned.
So let it guide us through the trials we face,
And lead us to a brighter, resilient embrace.

Love

In the depths of night, a soul does weep,
Love's tender touch turned into a bitter keep.
Trauma's cruel hand has left its mark,
Leaving a heart adrift in the dark.

Once a flame burning bright and true,
Now flickers faint, a shadow of its debut.
Lost in the labyrinth of memories untold,
Where love and trauma fiercely unfold.

The heart, a battlefield of scars and fears,
Echoes of laughter drowned in silent tears.
A love once cherished, now a haunting wraith,
Leaving the spirit adrift in its wretched scathe.

Yet in the midst of the desolate night,
A glimmer of hope, a beacon of light.
For love, though wounded, still holds its sway,
Guiding the lost back to the dawn of day.

Through the pain and the ache, a path will clear,
Where healing begins and love reappears.
Though lost and battered, the soul shall find,
A new dawn of love, gentle and kind.

So let the healing waters wash away the pain,
And love's gentle touch breathe life again.
For in the depths of trauma's chilling cost,
Love's resilience mends what once was lost.

Dirt roads

Upon the dirt roads, worn and old,
Where stories linger, yet untold,
Redemption waits with open arms,
In nature's embrace, where healing starts.

Beneath the sky's expansive dome,
The path winds on, calling us home,
To places where the soul finds peace,
And burdens fade, our hearts release.

Through fields of gold and meadows green,
The dirt road whispers, a timeless scene,
Of second chances, and a fresh start,
Where footprints mend a broken heart.

Each step we take, with faith in stride,
Leads us further from the pain we hide,
And as we walk, the dust may rise,
But so does hope, within our eyes.

For on these roads, both rough and kind,
Redemption's promise we may find,
In every turn, and every bend,
A chance to heal, a chance to mend.

So let's embrace the dirt roads' call,
And let redemption heal us all,
For in the earth, and in the sky,
Our souls find peace, and learn to fly.

Canyons

In canyons deep where shadows play,
I lost myself one fateful day.
Amidst the cliffs that touched the sky,
I wandered far, with no goodbye.

The winding paths led me astray,
Yet in that loss, I found my way.
The echoes of the ancient stone
Whispered secrets to me alone.

The rugged walls, both dark and grand,
Became the guides that helped me stand.
In solitude, I learned to see
The beauty in uncertainty.

The canyon's silence spoke so clear,
And brought to life my inner fear.
But through that fear, I found my voice,
And in its depths, I made my choice.

I let my worries drift like sand,
And reached out for the rugged land.
For in the canyons, wild and free,
I found the self I longed to be.

So if you're lost and feeling small,
Embrace the canyon's ancient call.
For in its depths, you may just find
The strength and peace to heal your mind.

Valleys

In the heart of the valleys, deep and wide,
Where shadows dance and whispers hide,
Lies the struggle of a timeless tale,
Of courage tested, and strength unveiled.

Through the winding paths, so steep and long,
The weary traveler sings a hopeful song,
For in the depths of the valley's embrace,
Lies the challenge that they must face.

The echoes of hardship, the cries of pain,
Resound through the mountains, like pouring
rain,
Yet through the darkness, a light still gleams,
Guiding the way to their wildest dreams.

Oh, valleys so vast, with trials untold,
Where the spirit is tested, and the heart grows
bold,
For in the struggle, we find our truth,
And discover within, the fountain of youth.

So let us journey through the valleys deep,
Where our faith is tested, and our souls do weep,
For in the struggle, we find our might,

And emerge from the darkness, into the glorious
light.

Country miles

Across the miles, I roamed with restless feet,
In search of what would make my spirit whole.
Through valleys deep and mountains stark and
steep,
I journeyed on to find my missing soul.

I wandered 'neath the blazing sun's bright gaze,
And danced with shadows in the pale moon's
light.
Through ancient cities lost in time's haze,
I sought the truth that would restore my sight.

I listened to the whispers of the wind,
And learned the wisdom of the ocean's song.
In every place, a piece of me I'd find,
As I traveled, feeling I did belong.

Through fields of gold and forests dark and
deep,
I sought the missing part to make me whole.
And in the end, when I had ceased to weep,
I found my soul within my very soul.

Forest shadows

In the heart of the ancient wood,
Where the trees stand tall and good,
Lies a place of childhood wonder,
Lost and found, hidden under.

In the dappled light, a secret waits,
A world of make-believe and fates,
Where fairies dance and spirits play,
In the forest's embrace, they find their way.

Once upon a time, a child did roam,
Amidst the trees, she found a home,
A place of magic, untouched by time,
Where innocence and joy intertwine.

Through the tangled vines and ferns,
She wandered, her heart begins to yearn,
For the dreams she left behind,
In this haven, she's sure to find.

In the whispering leaves, a melody,
Guides her back to what used to be,
The laughter, the games, the pure delight,
Lost in the woods, now shining bright.

As she rediscovers her long-lost treasure,
Her spirit lifts, she finds her pleasure,
In the simple joys of childhood's lore,
In the forest, she's lost no more.

So let us heed the forest's call,
Where childhood wonder waits for all,
Amidst the trees, we'll find our way,
And reclaim the magic of yesterday.

Time

In the heart of rolling hills so fair,
Where the river winds without a care,
Lies a place of tranquil, serene delight,
Where nature's beauty takes its flight.

The hills roll on in gentle grace,
Embracing the land in a warm embrace,
Their verdant slopes and golden fields,
A peaceful sanctuary that nature yields.

The river flows with a soothing song,
Its waters meander and drift along,
Reflecting the sky in shimmering light,
A timeless dance, both day and night.

Amidst this scene of tranquil repose,
The soul finds peace, and worries decompose,
As whispers of wind through grasses sigh,
And the cares of the world just pass on by.

So let us seek this serene domain,
Where the rolling hills and the river reign,
And find a moment of pure tranquility,
In nature's embrace, forever free.

Becoming me

Unbecoming to become

I shed the layers, one by one,
Unraveling the threads I've spun,
A metamorphosis, a sacred art,
Revealing the whispers of my heart.

I unbecome the roles I've played,
The masks I wore, the dues I've paid,
Stripping bare, I stand in grace,
Embracing truth in every trace.

I release the fears that held me tight,
Dissolving shadows, let in the light,
Breaking free from chains of old,
Discovering treasures left untold.

In letting go, I find the key,
To unlock the door and set me free,
To become the one I'm meant to be,
Embracing my authenticity.

So here I stand, stripped and bare,
In the rawness, I find my flair,
Unbecoming to become, I see,
The truest version of being me.

www.ingramcontent.com/pod-product-compliance
Lightning Source LLC
La Vergne TN
LVHW021346200726
843509LV00014B/2697